UNCONSIDERED TRIFLES

Images of the everyday for modellers and artists

by

GEOFF KENT

WILD SWAN BOOKS LTD.

Stretching all the way from the mouth of the Dee in the north to the shore of the Severn Estuary in the south, the earthen rampart commissioned by King Offa of Mercia in the eighth century to mark the western boundary of his realm could scarcely be called a 'trifle', but thirteen centuries on, even when it's highlighted by low October sunshine, you could be forgiven for not realising that this is indeed a remaining part of that vast monument to human ambition and endeavour. In fact, if my Ordnance Survey map hadn't told me to look out for it, I might not have noticed that I was driving past this well-preserved section of Offa's Dyke snaking across the uplands between the valleys of the Rivers Clun and Teme to the north of Knighton. Ample proof, incidentally, that a good map – and O.S. ones are far and away the best – tells you much more about your surroundings than any sat-nav ever could.

INTRODUCTION

For many years now I've made a habit of carrying a camera around to record anything and everything that reminds me of times not long past, especially those lesser man-made features of our environment that tend to come and go without our really noticing them, at least until they've gone. For the most part these are everyday, unremarkable things that were commonplace from Victorian times into the second half of the last century, but which have since been swept away by the constant tide of modernisation. Except, that is, for the odd survivals that I've tried to note before it's too late.

My fascination with these things grew out of my hobby of building transport models, both road and railway ones, and my conviction that every aspect of a miniature scene should reflect as accurately as possible the period in which the models are set – in my case the mid-1950s. So in my travels I've kept my eyes open, not just for features that are purely transport-related, but also for signs, buildings and general paraphernalia that have lasted more or less unchanged since those times.

Almost without exception, I'm avoiding in these pages those living museums and preservation sites which, I'm the first to admit, do such a grand job in recreating evocations of bygone days. Rather, I want to illustrate some of the thousand and one things that anyone with eyes to see can still find in places to which you and I have ready access by road or footpath. Some of these are curious, some quite attractive, a few even rather impressive, but mostly they're the 'blink and you miss it' kind of stuff we've taken for granted all our lives, and hardly ever think about even when we notice them.

Taking my cue from Autolycus in 'The Winter's Tale', I like to think that I've become something of a latter-day 'snapper-up of unconsidered trifles'.

Almost all these pictures have either been taken in the last three or four years, or show subjects whose continued existence I've recently been able to confirm. You'll quickly realise that certain parts of the British Isles feature more often than others, especially my adopted home county of Shropshire and the Welsh Marches generally, together with parts of Yorkshire and Lincolnshire. This certainly shouldn't be taken to suggest that other areas are devoid of interest: far from it. Only that I'm less familiar with them. So if any of this strikes a chord, or, better, stimulates you to take a closer look at your own surroundings, all well and good. Record what you find now. It may not be there tomorrow.

Geoff Kent, 2020.

DEDICATION
To R. J.

Cover photo. *This photo seems to sum up in several ways the exercise in nostalgia that is the theme of this book. The former market hall in Craven Arms in Shropshire, to me a most attractive building in its own right – look at the polychromatic brickwork, enhanced by the painted sign – is now 'The Land of Lost Content', a museum of the day-to-day memories of yesteryear, taking its name from one small part of A. E. Housman's anthology of poems 'A Shropshire Lad'.*

Into my heart an air that kills
From yon far country blows
What are those blue remembered hills,
What spires, what farms are those?

That is the land of lost content,
I see it shining plain:
The happy highways where I went,
And cannot come again.

D.W.WALL & SON
FAMILY BUTCHERS
Locally Sourced
Traditional
BRITISH MEAT
Home of the
Original
LUDLOW SAUSAGE
HIGH CLASS
Locally Sourced, Traditional Breeds Grass, Fed Beef, Dry Hung And Matured For 28 Days, Full of Flavour
D W Wall & Son Home of the Original Ludlow Park Sausage
Home Made Faggots, Black Pudding Reg May Pork Pies
Local Free Range Pork
Local Venison

SIGNS OF THE TIMES

To the man or woman of a certain age, one of the most obvious ways in which our surroundings have changed in the last half-century or so is in the appearance of our town centres, not just architecturally but also in the style of shop frontages, the names of the traders, the products they sell, and how those products are promoted. Reminders of how things were are disappearing all the time, but the process, though continuous, is a gradual one, and tends to go unnoticed until occasionally we spot a once-familiar sign or advert that brings home some awareness of the degree of change that has taken place.

Sometimes it's just the decorative style of a shop front that triggers our memory. In an era when they are so often bland, plasticky and cheap-looking, it's refreshing to find one that retains a strong element of traditional presentation, such as the butcher's shop on the High Street in Ludlow. For sheer exuberance, however, it would be hard to beat the art-deco magnificence of this outfitters in Llandudno, which has clearly gone through several changes of ownership: the two photos were taken fifteen years apart, and the mosaic threshold recalls a yet earlier generation. The glazed canopy with its cast-iron columns is a Victorian feature that can still be found in a number of seaside and inland spa towns, and Llandudno has happily kept its fair share of these, helping to make it one of the country's most characterful and well-presented resorts.

By contrast, the village post office and stores in Willoughton, Lincs, although also in the style of an earlier generation, is unashamedly plain and unadorned. The photo was taken in 1995, but surprisingly the shop remains virtually unchanged a quarter of a century later. The enamel plate on the letterbox headed by the Georgian royal cypher is an increasingly rare survival, but not to the extent of the notice over the door, which reads, in progressively smaller capitals, Post Office; Money Order Office; Savings Bank; Insurance and Annuity Office.

As evidenced in Llandudno, it was once very common for the floors in shop entrances to be laid in mosaic form, embellished with the name of the owner(s). These are still quite common, but with the passage of time usually advertise firms, both local and national, that no longer exist. Thus the former Maypole branch in Ludlow recalls a network of grocery shops once familiar across the country. Likewise, this reminder of the nationwide chain of shoe retailers Freeman, Hardy & Willis, can still be seen in Gainsborough.

A notable exception to the rule, in that it still trades under its original name, is Rickards' ironmongery and hardware shop, also in Ludlow: both street entrances have the name both in gilt letters above the doorways and repeated in the thresholds below, in one case in mosaic tiling, and in the other in brass letters set into the surface.

The continued use of gates to close off the entrances out of hours is another traditional feature nowadays rarely found, also to be seen here at an old-established optician's premises in Chester, which feature in addition a distinctive 'illiterate' sign in the form of a giant pair of spectacles. Regrettably, a visit early in 2020 showed the premises vacant and awaiting redevelopment, but I'm including it as a timely reminder of the need to record these things when you see them. Not far away, however, is another old-established local business: John Woods, white-smith, locksmith and keysmith, whose trademark is prominently displayed on the wall above. As a Cestrian born and bred, I should perhaps know the significance of these two cast plates on an adjoining pair of houses in Whitefriars; maybe someone will tell me. My childhood memories of the street centre rather on Mr. Green's model railway emporium, and, less happily, on my dentist's surgery nearby, both now long gone.

Another shop front feature once commonly seen everywhere was the practice of sticking individual letters, advertising products on sale within, onto the windows. Rarely, however, did this go to the lengths still to be seen on another ironmonger's, Banfield's, in Tenbury Wells, Worcestershire. Although some displays are incomplete, at least four makers' names can be identified together with the wares they manufactured. Another sign of the times is that, as far as I know, none of these once well-known firms is still in being today.

Back in Gainsborough, this attractive sign set into the wall of a pub commemorates the name of a long-departed Grimsby brewer, whose many tied houses once served North Lincolnshire and extended into Yorkshire and Nottinghamshire. The Ship Hotel at Bawtry recalls not only the same brewery, but also the once-common habit of displaying its identity on the tiles of the roof.

Painted advertisements (so-called 'ghost signs') also preserve once well-known names, such as this one for Cheshire's Ales in Kidderminster. And who now remembers Peto Scott Television, (Dependable and Really Worth Looking Into) (facing page), other than people who pass by this gable end in Bradford?

Not far away in Drighlington this huge Larkspur soft drinks ad has recently been repainted, a favour also conferred on Bile Beans, which are still being promoted on this wall in York.

My photo of Mr. Oxtoby the painter and decorator's former premises, again in York, was taken in 2001, but a recent visit confirms that the attractive period raised lettering is still in place on what is now a hairdressing salon.

Above and facing page top. *Vanished cigarette brands are remembered too: these ads for Woodbines, Capstan, Gold Flake and Players have all outlasted the cull following the ban on such advertising, as has the one for Westminster Virginia (tipped or plain), again in Bradford, and a brand moreover that I've never heard of. This last sign has the added bonus of combining two completely different messages, one on top of the other, giving an enquiring mind the interesting puzzle of trying to differentiate the faded wording for Harrison the bootmaker from that for the cigarette ad.*

Above. *Driving through Ruthin in the Vale of Clwyd recently and stopping at a red traffic light, I spotted on the wall opposite, this fading sign for a onetime provision merchant, Mr. O. R. Owen, owner of the Railway Stores. Not only is the building no longer a grocery, there hasn't been a working railway within miles for over half a century either.*

Left. *Another 'two for the price of one', although in this case two versions of the same message, greets you as you enter Shrewsbury over the English Bridge on the eastern side of the town centre. Velocette motor cycles were a famous make well into the second half of the last century, but the popularity of the light vehicles called cyclecars had ebbed away by the 1930s.*

Finally, the dying art of painting signs directly onto the masonry of buildings is gloriously typified by this eye-catcher on Morecambe promenade. Notice the shading of the individual letters: three distinct colours, red, black and green for the main wording; just plain green for the rest, but look also at the sinuous undulation of the bottom line as it curves round the perfection of the pointing hand. Proper signwriting at its most individualistic.

ON THE ROAD

Most of us are familiar with the basic principle of our road-numbering system, by which primary and secondary routes are classified as 'A' and 'B' roads. But how many people know that when numbers were first applied around a century ago it was the intention to have 'C' and 'D' roads as well? The proposal was soon dropped, at least for public consumption, but not before a few county councils had actually begun to implement it, so that even today the occasional sign with a 'C' number can still be seen. Here are two, one in Lincolnshire and (opposite top) *one in Norfolk.*

When the numbering system came in, some economy-minded councils, rather than having new signs made, amended their existing finger posts simply by tacking the numbers onto them. Other changes or additions were sometimes made the same way, or more recently just by painting out features that no longer applied. Cheshire was particularly fond of these adaptations and later, unlike some authorities, didn't scrap all its old signs overnight when new-fangled specifications came in. Happily there has even been a resurgence of new, old-style finger posts in some areas in recent years.

A selection of surviving original signs in different parts of the country begins here with pointing hands and a lamp at Pelsall, West Midlands.

This page shows concrete post, wooden arms and a Notts County Council octagon at East Leake; added road numbers with a Radnorshire roundel, near Presteigne; and wooden arms on a black-painted post embellished with the name of the village and surmounted by a disc recalling one of the three historical sub-divisions of Lincolnshire - Lindsey, Kesteven and Holland.

In the early days of road signage, designs and materials varied from place to place. Clearly illustrating the origin of the term 'finger post', this Shropshire example dating from 1800 has cut-out place names in iron pointers mounted on a stone column.

By the time cycling, and then motoring, came in, cast-iron was being used, though to no national standard; this plate still adorns a wall not three miles away on the same road.

The AA and the RAC introduced an element of standardisation, borne out by these enamel signs in Ludlow, Bridgnorth and East Yorkshire, and the 1919 Ministry of Transport Act led to the establishment of both the road numbering system and the countrywide range of traffic signs that remained in use until the European style of signage became the rule in the mid-sixties.

Not many of the older signs now survive, but here's a couple of examples from Shropshire, one of which is in the later enamel, rather than cast, form, together with another (strangely discoloured) enamel one seen recently in Egham in Surrey. The 'road narrows' sign is notable in including the 'Single Track Road' plate, and retains in good condition the red triangle once universally applied to signs of this style.

More commonly, milestones in a variety of materials can still be seen all over the country, although they sometimes take a bit of spotting. Some are very old indeed, dating back to, and even beyond, the days of turnpike roads. At least three of these crudely engraved stones can be seen on a back road between Bishops Castle and Craven Arms in Shropshire. Today this is no more than a country lane, but it's the most direct route between the two, and in years past was, I'm sure, one of the old drovers' roads along which livestock was herded to market from Wales to cities in England, especially London. There couldn't have been many other folk who wanted to know the distance from a small town in the county of Salop all the way to the capital, but to nowhere in between!

By contrast, this obelisk in Craven Arms itself must be one of the most informative milestones anywhere. There are altogether thirty-six place names on the three engraved faces, some very local, but some much further afield, including such seemingly unlikely destinations as Exeter and Berwick-on-Tweed, at least for someone starting from south Shropshire.

Starting here and continuing overleaf: Other styles generally represent individual turnpike trusts or county councils; elegant cast-iron mileposts from Powys, Herefordshire, Norfolk, and Derbyshire represent these, together with a Bath Turnpike Trust boundary sign at the intriguingly-named Brass Knocker Bar.

NORTON CANON
PARISH
TO
HEREFORD
10
MILES
TO
KINGTON
9
MILES

1827
TURNPIKE·TRUST
CLAVERTON
COMBE

TO WELLS
TO NORWICH
5
MILES
27
MILES

Top left. *This distinctive concrete design was more recently widely used by Worcestershire County Council.* Top right. *Even slate has been used on occasions, as here in what used to be part of Denbighshire; note that the distance to Wales' highest waterfall, Pistyll Rhaeadr, is accurate to the nearest chain, or twenty-two yards! Elsewhere on our roads, dwindling examples of other older signage can sometimes be found.* Above. *As we've seen on many finger posts, black and white chequer was adopted to draw drivers' attention to particular features, including clearance restrictions, and to assist them in wartime blackout conditions. Bridge parapets at Hayton in Nottinghamshire, and (overleaf) on the A76 north of Dumfries illustrate these.*

Another aid to visibility, especially in the dark, was the use of tiny glass reflectors, as on these two signs in Cardiff and at Malpas in Cheshire.

Village signs like this one just over the Welsh border from Whitchurch (Salop) are of a style once common in many parts of the country; notice the mileages to centres in front of and behind the motorist. And purely imperial height warnings, as on this rare survivor on an arch over the B6160 at Bolton Abbey in Yorkshire, were once in use on overbridges just about everywhere.

Reverting to direction signs, these interesting groupings at Leominster and Bridgnorth (overleaf) (show further variations of older signage. The green-infilled 'Main Road' sign may well be unique; and the street nameplates, one in blue and white enamel and the other in cast-iron with a decorative pointing hand, are certainly far from commonplace. So too, incidentally, is painting the identity of commercial premises and products (in this case the Shakespeare Inn and Joule's Salop Ales) directly onto the fabric of the building: a welcome continuation of another long-established tradition.

The border between England and Wales follows a rather serpentine course around Shropshire. One curious result of this is that in the northern part of the county you can drive more or less due east for several miles – apparently away from Wales – before passing briefly into what used to make up a detached part of Flintshire. This elderly 'Welcome to Wales' sign, complete with its red dragon, faces west to greet you at the point where you enter the Principality, albeit from an unlikely direction, and for only a few short miles.

Petrol pumps have gone through an evolutionary cycle of their own since they were introduced a hundred years ago. One of the earliest I've seen is this distinctive pump set into a recess in a wall in Llanidloes in Mid-Wales, designed to be operated by working the lever to and fro. The cast lettering in the shield near the base reads 'HAMMOND VISIBLE PETROL SYSTEM MODEL', referring to the glazed display at the top of the column.

Of a more modern design, but once again manually operated in similar fashion, are these two pumps at the roadside in the village of Manafon in the Rhiw Valley in Powys. Finally, this closed garage at Much Wenlock exemplifies not only various pump designs, but also typical local petrol stations cum repair businesses of yesteryear.

And if you thought that all such roadside filling stations were things of the past, this is the hardware shop in Montgomery, where fuel is still dispensed over the pavement using the kind of pivoting pipe gantry that was once taken for granted anywhere and everywhere. Inside, Bunner's is one of those wonderful places with bare-boarded floors and rows of small drawers for every useful artefact known to man, where you can get from stock a new fire grate, a mole trap, a galvanised bucket, a single screw or nut and bolt, or, I have no doubt, a gas mantle should you ever need one. And old adverts still encourage discerning customers to buy indispensable things like a Jones sewing machine or a Lister stationary engine.

Apart from direction and traffic signs, something that both the AA and the RAC were also noted for was their roadside telephone boxes, a few of which have been preserved, including this one at Eardisland in Herefordshire. All members were issued with a key to use them to seek assistance, and this exclusivity was underlined when motorists displaying the appropriate badge were saluted by passing patrolmen on their motorcycle and sidecar combinations. Those were the days.

BUILDINGS AND STRUCTURES

Walling comes in a tremendous variety of forms. Perhaps the simplest – and oldest – is represented by this ancient stone slab boundary wall near Rhayader in Mid-Wales. Elsewhere in the Principality slate slabs were used in the same way.

Also of venerable age is the massive flint curtain wall of the former priory at Blakeney in north Norfolk, but even this is dwarfed by this towering retaining wall at Acrefair in the Vale of Llangollen. Not far away at Ffrwd north of Wrexham the bank alongside a sunken lane is held back by the more random dry block work of another retaining wall.

Rather more sophisticated building techniques are evident in these lime kilns, also in the Wrexham area at Minera and disused now for many decades. More modern construction in north-east Wales naturally makes great use of the brick products for which the area was famous for a century and more. Records indicate that the narrow industrial corridor stretching down through Flintshire and Denbighshire has over the years been host to well over a hundred brick-making sites. Still, the use of glazed bricks for simple things like this garden wall is relatively unusual. The range of colours achievable in this material is evidenced by the boundary wall of the former Tref-y-nant works of one of the area's largest manufacturers, J. C. Edwards.

The same maker's Pen-y-Bont works specialised in terracotta products, and has left this striking office-cum-gatehouse building, no doubt intended to advertise the company's capabilities to visitors and passers-by alike. Some idea of the versatility of this material may be gauged by this rather grand structure, the Westminster Coach and Motor Car Works as was, which still stands on the Market Square in Chester.

A terracotta winged creature decorating a building in Salisbuy and, on a more modest scale, this butcher's shop in the village of Tattenhall in Cheshire. Would I be right in thinking that the oval frame might once have borne a similar picture to this one to be seen above another butcher's premises in Shropshire?

Brick and tile production today is a far cry from the time when a multiplicity of small yards existed all over the country, wherever suitable clay could be found, to supply the needs of their immediate locality. But there are still a few works supplying niche markets, like Wm. Blyth's two tileries at Barton-on-Humber, Lincs, making pantiles. The two kilns, the chimneys, and the drying sheds are all very typical of the small-scale operations of yesteryear. Not many small, lock-up shops were as stylish as the one we've just seen in Tattenhall. Time was when many were cobbled together from materials like corrugated-iron, timber and roofing felt, but this roadside café on the outskirts of Brighouse, West Yorkshire, is nowadays quite a rare survivor. As the photos, taken a number of years apart, clearly show, the building has had a makeover, and now looks much smarter, though otherwise hardly changed. A touch of style is added by the steep gables with their finials and scalloped bargeboards, and the retention of folding shutters is something else you don't often see these days. As can be seen by the fenced-off embankment in the background, the Pickle Bridge Sandwich Hut (wonderful name!) was originally built in the shadow of a railway bridge, now demolished, a fate that has befallen many, many others across the country. But not all redundant bridges have gone the same way. The Rea Aqueduct is a case in point.

Little-known, even in its own locality, the Leominster Canal was a product of the Canal Mania of the late eighteenth century, but having failed to reach either its planned inland destination of Kington or its intended connection to the wider waterway network at Stourport on the Severn, it lived out its landlocked life on the verge of bankruptcy until being finally closed in 1860 for a railway to be built over part of its course. But for an insignificant canal that never performed as hoped, and ceased to function entirely more than a century and a half ago, it has nonetheless left its mark on the countryside: in particular, there are substantial remains of a tunnel and two aqueducts, one of these being this crumbling, but still impressive, brick arch over the River Rea not far from its eastern terminus near Mamble in Worcestershire. Unlike most of the images in this album, the Rea Aqueduct isn't readily visible to someone who's not looking for it, though there is a public right-of-way across it, and I've included it as a reminder of some of the more dramatic, if hidden, remnants of our industrial history.

Even so, it's easy at this distance to forget that the Leominster Canal did fulfil a need of sorts for well over fifty years. Another feature of nineteenth century transport that had a much shorter life before being abandoned, but which can still be seen at the side of a road in North Yorkshire is this handsome stone bridge near Goathland. It was built to carry the Whitby & Pickering Railway, opened in 1835, over a farm track. Conceived as a horse-worked line, it wasn't long before steam traction was being seen as a necessary development, but as built it included a steep incline which locomotives could not climb. So in 1865 a deviation line (now a section of the North Yorkshire Moors Railway) was constructed on easier gradients by-passing the incline and parts of both the upper and lower levels of the original route, including this bridge. But such were the standards employed in the earlier work by the line's engineer, George Stephenson, that the bridge, apparently in the middle of nowhere, has lasted in very respectable condition to this day.

A bridge of similar vintage is this simple, but impressive, suspension span over the River Ancholme in Lincolnshire. The reason for such a grand structure is a little obscure today: Horkstow Bridge is at the end of a country lane, and the tarmac ends where the wooden deck begins. Only an unmade track, officially no more than a bridleway, continues on the far side. Still, no doubt in Victorian times it was more than adequate for carts, livestock, and people on foot or horseback. Even today it boasts a three-tonne weight limit.

Of course, suspension bridges large and small are common enough, but I know of only one built solely to take a footpath over a railway, namely this one over the line between Crewe and Shrewsbury. It once crossed several tracks near Whitchurch Station, hence its length, but now there are only two.

At Nantwich Station the same line is fortunate in having another distinctive footbridge. Though sadly cluttered by all that modern palisade fencing, this long iron lattice structure spans the tracks at the level crossing at the end of the platforms.

Road bridges built of iron date back to the 1700s: the famous forerunner at Ironbridge in the Severn Gorge was opened in 1781. A fine later example, also over the Severn, and still in use for today's traffic, is at Abermule. The cast wording proudly reads 'THIS SECOND IRON BRIDGE CONSTRUCTED IN THE COUNTY OF MONTGOMERY WAS ERECTED IN THE YEAR 1852'. Immediately next to it, this much more modest structure carries the road on over the Montgomeryshire Canal. The plate commemorates the fact that the beams were cast at Brymbo Ironworks in the following year. The brick pillar added to support heavier traffic would have been an inconvenience to horse-drawn canal traffic, at least if it was there before the mid-1930s, when the already little-used waterway fell out of use completely.

A rather more stylish canal bridge that makes up for its limited span by the neat simplicity of its iron arch and railings between brick and stone abutments, has crossed the Wirral Arm of the erstwhile Ellesmere Canal near Upton-by-Chester since 1795.

We're inclined to think of timber trestle bridges as features of railroads in the Wild West, but early railways in Britain had them as well. Most have been replaced in iron and masonry over the years, but this one in the Wye Valley combining iron beams beneath the rails with a supporting structure of stout timber baulks is unusual in having outlived the railway it carried by fifty years and more.

The British Isles are fortunately rich in small and medium-sized country towns, and nearly all have something to offer the seeker after reminders of times past. One such is Tenbury Wells in Worcestershire, whose neat little circular market hall is something of a gem. We've already looked at the frontage of Banfield's, the ironmongers, and a notable quirk is the town's six-arch bridge over the River Teme, which has a pronounced bend in the middle. But as its name implies, Tenbury once had aspirations of becoming a major spa town, and even if it never grew to rival Bath, Harrogate or Cheltenham, it did succeed in giving us quite the most extraordinary structure illustrated in these pages, namely its wonderfully eccentric Pump Rooms. Everything about the building is startling, from the neo-half-timbering and its effect on the window outline to the arched polychromatic brick and stonework around the entrance that contrasts so markedly with the rest of the fabric. Even the detail work, like the elaborate ridge tiling and the decorative railings at the front, is noteworthy. But most astonishing of all is surely that fantastic, slender, metal-lapped spire.

Turning to domestic architecture, these three examples, all from Wales, are particularly distinctive, I feel. The first is a pair of properties in Llanidloes, far from identical except in the generous use of coloured brickwork and the matching design of their garden railings. They're notable too in the retention of traditional sash windows throughout, while the wrought-iron porch of the farther one, and the stone quoins of the nearer, are other pleasing features. The slate-hung gables of the adjoining buildings typify a common weather-proofing technique in this part of the world.

Multi-coloured brick on the frontage and tall chimneys of this half of a pair of semi-detached villas in Mold presents a similarly striking effect, contrasting with the slightly surprising random stonework of the side wall. The detail of the bargeboards on the gables, together with their finials, contributes well to the whole.

Very different is this archetypal 1930s property in Rhos-on-Sea. Few buildings of the period retain so complete a display of the revolutionary, but short-lived, design features of that decade, even down to the door and the railings.

Even fewer industrial buildings have survived well from the 1930s, but the gatehouse/office of the former lime works, now a haulage and storage depot, at Hibaldstow in Lincolnshire retains the rounded corners, curved windows and flat roof so redolent of the period, together with some nice, traditionally-styled signwriting. Turning ninety degrees to the right you would see another characterful structure, the tall signal box of Kirton Lime Sidings shown elsewhere. And at least two blocks of old kilns still exist nearby alongside the railway line.

Pub architecture achieved something of a pinnacle of style and elaboration in Victorian times, as demonstrated by these three examples. The brick and tiled frontage of The Elephant and Castle in Wakefield is almost monumental, whereas that of The White Lion in Sheffield is more subdued, but excels in the artistic design of its leaded glass windows with their inset lettering - notice the reversed N in the farther one.

The striking stucco work on the gable of The Old Three Tuns in Wrexham is beautifully complex: the horse's head at the top recalls, I believe, the Nag's Head Brewery, now like both of the others advertising a name from days long past. Non-conformist chapels offer a wide variety of architecture, from the very grand to the very simple. Two of my favourites in the latter category are the quite domestically-styled one at Carmel in mid-Wales and the almost equally understated example at Stottesdon in Shropshire (opposite top).

More imposing is the naïve classical frontage of the former Bethel Welsh Congregational Chapel at Rhosymedre near Ruabon; the little red brick vestry tacked on at the side adds a down-to-earth touch.

This leads us nicely into that most underrated of architectural materials, corrugated-iron, much used in years past for chapels, village halls, meeting rooms, etc. Regrettably, too many of these are now as down-at-heel as this sad example at Dolyhir in Radnorshire as was. Others are more cherished, however: the church of St. John the Baptist at Maesbury, near Oswestry, is a perfect instance. Moreover, it's one of the few remaining full-blown parish churches in this material. Another is the village hall, deservedly Grade II listed, at Llanddewi Skirrid near Abergavenny.

But in its heyday corrugated-iron saw a much greater range of applications, in industry, agriculture and transport, for instance, and not least in housing. Two examples of this, both still occupied, are these dwellings at Ditton Priors, Shropshire, and Immingham, Lincs (still known locally as Tin Town, from the many semi-permanent iron buildings that mushroomed during the building of the deep-water dock in the early 1900s).

Living accommodation of a rather different kind is illustrated by these Nissen huts at Fillingham, also in Lincolnshire, relics of a wartime RAF base. Crinkly tin has also been used as a cheap and cheerful re-roofing material, sometimes over thatch, though apparently not in the case of this cottage at Bulkeley in Cheshire.

Making considerable use of corrugated-iron for both roofing and gate panelling are the premises of Messrs. Jones & Sons, builders merchants, in Llanfyllin, Powys, otherwise a nicely symmetrical and well-maintained combination of timber and glass above brick footings, the two wings differing in only minor details.

All the same, many people's awareness of the uses of the material stops short at sheds and barns. Even here, though, there is considerable variety to be seen. In its time, one of the largest bus companies in the country, serving Merseyside, much of Cheshire, and most of north and mid-Wales, was Crosville Motor Services, which had a particular liking for corrugated-iron for many of its lesser depots, including this one at Machynlleth, as seen here in Arriva's hands.

Contrasting with this, a tiny shed in rural Shropshire, a sort of shepherd's hut without wheels, contrives to exhibit, with its finials, decorative ridge and pierced bargeboards, an unexpected degree of style for so unassuming a structure.

Finally, an attractive feature of iron buildings, especially barns and the like, is the commonly seen cast, pressed or enamelled plate advertising the maker's name. A few from different parts of the country are reproduced here.

RAILWAY MATTERS

The country's railway network has changed almost beyond recognition in my lifetime, and reminders of how it used to be are declining day-by-day. Happily, the process is not yet complete, and it can be a revealing exercise to seek out such reminders in the most unlikely places. Just such an unexpected surprise was finding this elderly lattice footbridge carrying a footpath between fields over the four tracks of the modern, electrified West Coast main line at Old Linslade in Bedfordshire. Some areas are more rewarding than others however. For a real railway time-warp, try north Lincolnshire. What was once part of the main line of the Manchester, Sheffield & Lincolnshire Railway, the stretch between Gainsborough and Barnetby still boasts five traditional signal-boxes, two of them with proper level-crossing gates. The long gates at Brigg are particularly impressive, the result of a wide main road crossing the line on the skew. The tall, timber-built box at Kirton Lime Sidings owes its unusual dimensions to the need for the signalman to see over the adjoining road bridge.

But it's the Barton-on-Humber branch that really takes us back. Again, there are three signal boxes, all with gated level-crossings, two of them at New Holland barely a quarter of a mile apart. A further crossing over a by-road is still hand-operated, and one of the six stations (on a rural line less than ten miles long) retains nameboards with separate letters, a style now almost extinct on the national network. Pride of place must go to Goxhill: the original station building is in private hands, but to see the signal-box (complete with its red LNER trespass warning sign), signals and gates is like taking a step back in time. But even Bystaple Lane Crossing is well worth a visit. Although the crossing-keeper's cottage is no longer occupied, the keeper being housed in a portacabin, the well-kept gates, the road surface of old sleepers, and that telegraph pole (albeit minus wires) make it hard to believe that we're not looking at a 'preserved' railway. For how much longer, though, I wonder.

Not that other locations are completely devoid of interest. These unusual (?unique) signals at Shrewsbury certainly attract attention, especially against the background of the largest remaining mechanical signal-box in the country.

A few miles away at Rednal on the line to Chester is this timber-built goods shed in sound original condition over half a century since it passed out of railway use. Stone- and brick-built ones are almost ten-a-penny (some, like Kidderminster, proclaiming the name of the railway company that owned them prior to nationalisation in 1948), but how many all-wooden sheds survive? Not many, I think.

While we're at Rednal, this anonymous little brick and timber building alongside the restored Montgomery Canal not far from the site of the railway station is said to be the interchange point for the short-lived 'swift' horse-drawn canal passenger service from Newtown and Welshpool before they were themselves railway-served, enabling people to reach the outside world more quickly than ever before, at least by mid-nineteenth century standards. Beside it is another reminder of pre-mechanically-powered canal transport, an ingenious 'turnover' or 'roving' bridge by which a boat horse could cross the water wherever the towpath changed sides without its towline having to be detached. Notice how the end of the wall is smoothly shaped to allow the rope to slip onto or off it without snagging. At one time, Rednal also boasted a rail/canal goods exchange basin; it was indeed something of an unlikely transport hub in the middle of the Shropshire countryside.

In case you think we're straying from the railway theme, this canal, and many others, came to be owned by a railway company, in this case the London & North Western Railway. But not before it had itself, unlike most other canals, also taken to building railways, in particular the line from Stafford to Wellington, grandly renaming itself in the process the Shropshire Union Railways & Canal Company, as commemorated by this restored sign at the canal basin in Ellesmere.

Most self-respecting railway goods depots had a cart weighbridge and the small cabins, now disused, that housed the weighman and his equipment can still sometimes be found. This example at Eastoft on the Fockerby branch of the former Axholme Joint Railway became redundant when the line closed to goods traffic in 1965. A more unlikely survival is the wooden shed glimpsed in the background: this is the station waiting room, unused for that purpose since 1933, when the branch passenger service ceased. The weighing facility at Church Stretton, also long disused, is unusual on two counts: first, the cabin, which survives, is built of timber, rather than the more common brick or stone (although since the photo was taken twenty years ago the ivy has enveloped it completely, making it all but unrecognisable for what it is). Second, the weigh table itself hasn't been removed; not only that, it's set in the surface of the roadway to the old station building, now in other hands, with nothing to prevent traffic from driving over it or parking on it.

Another feature of railway stations large and small was (and often still is) a proliferation of railings, fences and gates. This extensive, if rather garish, colonnade at Caergwrle between Wrexham and Birkenhead is characteristic of the pattern adopted by several railway companies, in this case the one-time Great Central Railway. Just visible in the background is this wooden gate which once closed off a private siding, and now stands isolated at the side of the line. The siding itself was removed around seventy(!) years ago.

The Barton-on-Humber branch that we've already looked at was also part of the Great Central. The platform railings at Thornton Abbey are of a different, but no less attractive, pattern, dating back to Victorian times, adding to the effect of the nameboard with its individual letters. The imposing gatehouse of the medieval abbey that gives the station its name can just be seen above the trees in the distance, perhaps a more conventional, though still relatively unsung, attraction to visitors to this corner of Lincolnshire.

This distinctive gate marked the entrance to the former Misterton Station on the line between Gainsborough and Doncaster. The station building is now in private hands, but the retention and continued use of the original gate, again of a venerable age, is remarkable. Notice, too, the heavy castings holding the tie-rods bracing the ironwork of the unusually long gate.

Most railway companies were happy to save money by re-using materials made redundant by old age or modernisation. The Great Western used large quantities of this early pattern of rail in many miles of its lineside post-and-wire fencing. The rail used for this straining post has clearly lasted much better than the concrete ones beyond it.

Cattle pens were found at many country and market town stations, but very few original ones can be seen today. An exception is the large range at Welshpool. Heavily overgrown for many years, the site has recently been cleared, and although the pens themselves aren't in perfect condition, their design is clear for all to see. The railway siding beside the pens, flush-surfaced in concrete to make cleaning easier in what could be a rather noisome environment, is a rare original example in this country of dual-gauge trackwork. The three rails were there to accommodate both the standard gauge of the main line and the narrow gauge of the Welshpool & Llanfair Railway. The W&L is now happily in preservation, but has lost the mile or so of its route through the town that once brought it to its terminus close to the main line station, thus isolating this small but significant remnant of its history.

A final reminder of times past on the railways is this well-preserved platelayers' cabin alongside the route of the line from Llanidloes and Builth Wells to Brecon, closed in 1962. Such simple buildings, here constructed, apart from the chimney, from old sleepers and corrugated-iron, could once be found every few miles along all lines, the homes of lengthmen whose daily duty it was to patrol each yard of track checking for faults, keeping down lineside growth, maintaining drains, fencing, gates and so on. The bodies of old railway vehicles, and indeed of old buses and trams, have long been considered as useful sheds, static caravans, or even as permanent homes, though their numbers are declining almost by the day. Few have been kept in the condition of this carriage body at Llangranog on the coast of Cardigan Bay, and few early vehicles of any kind have survived as completely as this one in Lincolnshire.

Grounded railway goods vans are still fairly numerous, but most are now much younger than this example, which dates back to the early years of the last century. Unlikely as it seems, it's one of only two built to carry gunpowder for the Cambrian Railways at Oswestry in 1905. When I first spotted it twenty-odd years ago, the running number W101633 was still just decipherable, but now the only obvious signs of its identity and purpose are the cast plate on the door (NOTICE. NO UNAUTHORISED PERSON IS ALLOWED TO OPEN THESE DOORS), and above it the faintly visible remains of part of the large red cross that the Great Western Railway used to highlight its gunpowder vans before nationalisation in 1948. Although it enjoyed a long life on the rails – over fifty years, in fact – it has now lain gently rusting in a Shropshire field for even longer.

Somewhat newer, but still nearly ninety years old, this steel container, a forerunner of the rather larger boxes that are in use everywhere today, was built for the London & North Eastern Railway in 1932. Lying alongside the line of the preserved North Yorkshire Moors Railway, but apparently not on railway land, it's to be hoped that it has already been earmarked for recovery and restoration before long.

THIS, THAT AND THE OTHER

The first photograph might be said to provide something of a bridge from the previous section, in that these two traditionally-styled lamp standards are on railway property in Shrewsbury. The swan necks with their cast decoration are complemented by the plain, but distinctly period, shades.

Of a very similar pattern, this example at Cefn, near Ruabon, illustrates in addition the way in which the base of the tapering column can also be enhanced by additional complex moulding. Lamp standards of this vintage may still be seen about the country, but have usually been fitted with more modern lighting equipment, as this one has in a limited way.

Another once common design with a double dished reflector is typified by these lamps at Bewdley, Worcs, and (overleaf) *Saltaire, West Yorkshire.*

The second example is at the huge mill complex developed by Titus Salt, and is mounted on the wall alongside the public road leading past what is now a gallery-cum-shopping centre. Also visible from the road is a blue police lamp, although the one illustrated is actually on the frontage of Shrewsbury Station (railway, not police), whose ornate stonework is a testament to the architectural skills of our Victorian forebears.

We've already looked at signage of one sort or another, and here are a few more that I've come across recently, including this rather attractive Cyclists Touring Club roundel, high up on the gable of the Herbert Arms at Chirbury, Shropshire.

Even in less-than-perfect condition, enamel advertising plates are much sought after, and few remain in their original position these days, so this survivor on a former smithy in Lincolnshire is something of a rarity.

Elsewhere, this reminder of the late, lamented (?) News of the World *in Montgomery has found a new role as a community notice board.*

In the days before it became normal for private homes to have a telephone, certain places, particularly post offices and railway stations, offered a public phone service as advertised by this sign on a wall in mid-Wales. A telephone sign of a different sort is this one bracketed off an electricity pole in rural Shropshire. Perhaps it owes its continued existence partly to being concealed for much of the year by the foliage that has grown up around it. It is nonetheless still relevant: public call boxes may be dwindling, but the one it relates to is in fact a quarter of a mile away in the direction indicated.

Brass plates identifying the (often professional) owners or occupiers of various premises also seem to be much thinner on the ground than they once were, and were in any case generally less striking than this one in Dublin. The more typically modest example from Leominster, Herefordshire, is accompanied by two different water hydrant signs, the upper one of a distinctly earlier style than the modern version below it.

Some patterns of gates and railings have been seen in relation to railway infrastructure, but they do, of course, enjoy a much wider range of applications. This field gate at Tedsmore (Salop), with its attendant kissing gate – a public footpath crosses the field – is simple but attractive; the lichen colonizing the massive post adds a colourful touch. Rather more elaborate is this well-kept gateway near Brigg, Lincs incorporating flanking railings, tall cast fluted posts and a wicket gate. Notice that the gaps between the horizontal bars narrow towards the bottom, a common feature reflecting the need to contain both large animals and smaller ones. Also in Lincolnshire, the gate into the churchyard at Pilham, although on a smaller scale, displays a pleasing variation of style, particularly in the design of the posts with their unusual impression of spiral bindings and their heavy spherical cappings.

An entirely different kind of church gateway is the lychgate of the parish church at Stokesay in Shropshire. This and the mounting block to its right were the real reason for taking the photograph, but the east window of the church itself and the half-timbered gatehouse of Stokesay Castle (strictly speaking not a castle at all, but a medieval fortified manor house) may be glimpsed in the background.

Finally, on the subject of gates, this slightly careworn garden gate at Westbury, near Shrewsbury, has intricately-cast posts bearing the name of the foundry at Coalbrookdale, birthplace of the Industrial Revolution.

Bollards to discourage road vehicles from mounting pavements have been around for at least two centuries. Early ones often used old cannon barrels, and that general shape was stylised or simplified as time went on, though commonly retaining the half-round cannon ball in the muzzle, like the furthest one of this group in Pembridge, Herefordshire. All three are quite different: most distinctive is the bell-shaped one in the middle. Once again, painting them black and white to aid visibility is a traditional precaution.

Most horse and cattle troughs that still exist generally fulfil other purposes today, like this one at Craven Arms. Many were inscribed with a form of the wording seen here: care for our animals is nothing new. The other side reads 'The Metropolitan Drinking Fountain and Cattle Trough Association', which supplied it and many others.

Cellar doors set into the pavement are still numerous, especially outside pubs – or former pubs – but less so bearing clear evidence of their age and origins. It's a sobering thought that up to ten generations of Ludlovians have walked over this pair since they were installed, yet the name of C. Hodges of Ludlow, and the date 1846, are still clearly visible on both leaves. But how many people in all those years, I wonder, have noticed this?

In the days before the majority of homes were connected to a piped water supply, most people's drinking water had to be fetched from a standpipe or the village pump. This one, dated 1876, stands in the centre of Montgomery, Powys.

Although the coal merchant at Haworth, West Yorkshire, still works out of the former goods yard at the station on the preserved Keighley & Worth Valley Railway, he no longer receives his coal by rail. But he does use this traditional set of weigh scales when filling the sacks he takes to his customers.

These iron tubs were spotted on a farm near Wrexham a decade or so ago. Similar ones were formerly used with cranes for coaling railway engines and for discharging bulk materials such as ores from ships in port. Notice the hinged clips that hold the hooped handles upright until the time comes to tip out the contents. Loading the tubs was of course done by manual labour.

And if you've ever wondered what a naked cat's eye looks like (hasn't everyone?), then look no further. Is it just me, or does it vaguely suggest some bottom-feeding sea creature caught out of its native element?